50 STATES TO CELEBRATE

Celebrating
FLORIDA

www.hmhbooks.com

The text of this book is set in Weidemann.
The display type is set in Bernard Gothic.
The illustrations are drawn with pencil and colored digitally.
The maps are pen, ink, and watercolor.

Photograph of Florida panther on page 32 © 2013 by U.S. Fish and Wildlife Service, George
    Gentry
Photograph of mockingbird on page 32 © 2013 by Michael Stubblefield/Alamy
Photograph of orange blossom on page 32 © 2013 by Randolph Femmer/National Biological
    Information Infrastructure

Library of Congress Cataloging-in-Publication Data
Bauer, Marion Dane.
Celebrating Florida / by Marion Dane Bauer ; illustrated by C. B. Canga.
p. cm. — (Green light readers level 3) (50 states to celebrate)
ISBN 978-0-547-89699-1 (paper over board)
ISBN 978-0-547-89698-4 (trade paper)
1. Florida—Juvenile literature. I. Canga, C. B. II. Title.
F311.3.B38 2013
975.9—dc23
2012016886

Manufactured in China
SCP 10 9 8 7 6 5 4 3 2 1
4500395315

50 STATES TO CELEBRATE

Celebrating
FLORIDA

Written by **Marion Dane Bauer**
Illustrated by **C. B. Canga**

sandpiper

Houghton Mifflin Harcourt
Boston   New York   2013

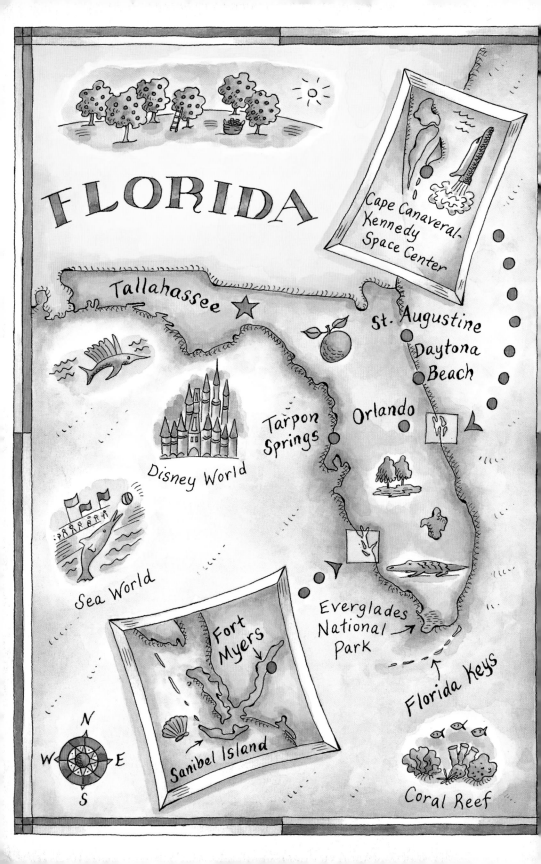

Hi! I'm Mr. Geo.

Here I am in the Sunshine State.

Do you know which state that is?

That's right . . . Florida!

More than 80 million people visit Florida each year.

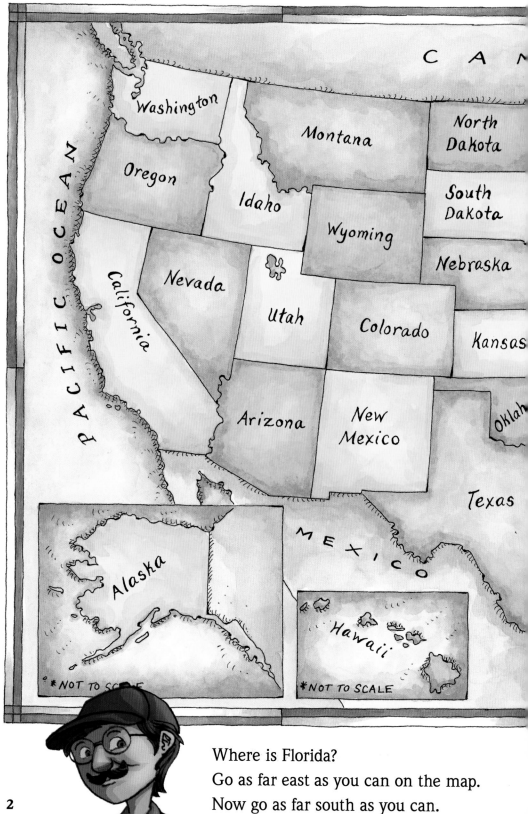

Where is Florida?
Go as far east as you can on the map.
Now go as far south as you can.

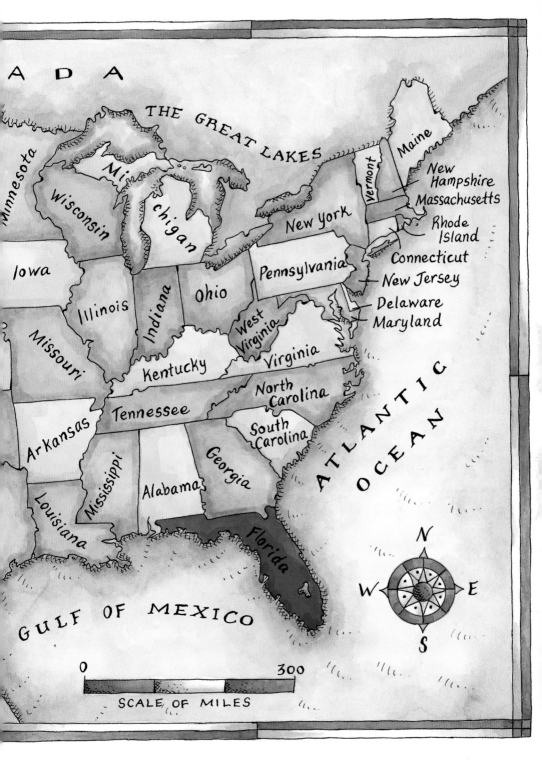

See that long **peninsula** sticking out
into the ocean?
That's Florida.

Come with me on an **airboat** ride through one of the largest **swamps** in the country. That swamp is in the **Everglades.**

We skim between mangrove trees.
We dance through water lilies.

From the airboat we see wildlife close up.

Alligators and crocodiles!

Pelicans and flamingos!

Egrets and bald eagles!

Bears and deer!

Look! A panther!
What a rare and wonderful sight!

Florida is the only known place in the world where crocodiles and alligators **coexist.**

Now let's go to the coast.
We can see **manatees** and dolphins there.

Did you know?

Manatees are so gentle that they
sometimes swim close to snorkelers.

Fort Myers Beach has sugary white sands.

It hosts a sand-sculpting contest every year.

Did you make that mermaid?

Sanibel Island is one of the greatest places
in the world to go seashelling.
Come with me during low tide.
Remember to bring a bucket or net.

You will find scallops, sand dollars, lightning whelks, conch shells, and much more. You'll even find egg cases from lightning whelks. They look like snakes!

Florida is a great place to play.
People come from everywhere
to visit Walt Disney World.
Cinderella's castle is my favorite.

And I love parades, fireworks, and . . . posing with Mickey Mouse!

There are other fun theme parks too.
Would you like to meet a black and white
whale named Shamu?
At SeaWorld, that's exactly what I did!

At Universal Orlando, we can walk into
movies and books that we love.
I just saw the Cat in the Hat!
And look at all the people who want to fly
with Harry Potter. I do too!

Florida is a great place to pick a fresh orange.

Or a juicy grapefruit.

Or a fat, ripe strawberry.

Florida grows more oranges than any other state. The only place in the world that grows more oranges is the country of Brazil.

And don't forget to visit Tarpon Springs,
the **sponge** capital of the world.
I want to take a sponge home
with me to use in my bath.

A sponge looks like a plant,
but it is actually an animal that lives
deep in the ocean.

In Florida, I can watch my favorite
baseball team in spring training.
Do you have a team you like best?
They probably come here to practice too.
Today, I'm cheering for Florida's
hometown teams.
Go Rays! Go Marlins!

Florida has its own professional teams in football, basketball, and hockey, too. And many people come here especially for golf, tennis, and auto racing.

Did you know?

Go-carts, motorcycles, stock cars, and sports cars all race at Daytona International Speedway.

19

When I visit someplace new,
I like to see something old.
In Florida, I visit the oldest city
in the United States, St. Augustine.

St. Augustine was settled more than 50 years
before the Pilgrims landed at Plymouth Rock.

Juan Ponce de León from Spain explored Florida in 1513.

Many say he was looking for gold and treasure.

Legends say he was searching for a **mythical Fountain of Youth.**

What he found was a land of flowers, La Florida.

Don't these orange blossoms smell sweet?

But the very first people in Florida were Native Americans.

In the east, there were the **Ais** and **Tequesta**.

In the west, the **Tocobaga** and **Calusa**.

Today, the **Seminole** stand strong, proud, and free. They honor old customs and brave leaders such as **Osceola.**

You can experience Seminole food, music, storytelling, and dance at the Florida Folk Festival.

Different countries fought to own the land.
Pirates prowled the seas.
Hurricanes wrecked ships.
Many people died of tropical illnesses and fevers.

Did you know?

At the St. Augustine Pirate and Treasure Museum you can see real pirate gold . . . and pirate swords, too!

Pirate ships no longer roam the coast of Florida.

But there are still hurricanes!

Hurricanes bring rain, wind, and high waves.

I even met a **tornado** there once.

Although Florida has strong storms,
it is a great place to live.
The weather is often sunny and warm.
But there is also lots of rain to help everything grow.
Together, the sun and rain feed millions of acres
of timberland.

Besides being nearly surrounded by ocean,
Florida has thousands of lakes and water **springs.**
Sailing, anyone?

Let's splash our way
to the first underwater state park
in the United States.
It's a coral reef in the **Florida Keys.**
We can **scuba dive** or **snorkel** or look underwater
through a glass-bottom boat.

The water in the Keys is clear and many
pretty shades of blue and green.
It is home to hundreds of different kinds of fish.
See this fish I caught?

But there is something else I've always wanted to do.
The Kennedy Space Center at Cape Canaveral is
the place to do it.
We have sent men to the moon from here.
We have sent a robotic explorer to Jupiter.

The first launch from Cape Canaveral was
on July 24, 1950. The rocket, Bumper 8,
rose ten miles into the air.

Now I'm ready to zoom there too.
Would you like to join me?
10 . . . 9 . . . 8 . . . 7 . . . 6 . . . 5 . . . 4 . . . 3 . . .
2 . . . 1 . . .
BLASTOFF!

Fast Facts About Florida

Nickname: The Sunshine State, because the sun shines most of the time.

State motto: In God we trust.

State capital: Tallahassee.

Other major cities: Jacksonville, Miami, Orlando, Tampa.

Year of statehood: 1845.

State animal: Florida panther.

State bird: Mockingbird.

State flower: Orange blossom.

State flag:

Population: Just under 19 million, according to the 2010 U.S. census.

Fun fact: Nearly 1,000 people move to Florida every day!

Dates in Florida History

600–1500: Native Americans in Florida begin farming and forming permanent villages.

1513: Juan Ponce de León from Spain is the first European to land in Florida.

1565: St. Augustine becomes the first permanent European settlement in what is now the United States.

1763: Spain gives Florida to Britain.

1783: Spain regains control of Florida.

1817: First of three Seminole Wars begins.

1821: Florida officially becomes a territory of the United States.

1845: Florida becomes the 27th state of the United States.

1885: Business people start building railroads and hotels in Florida.

1912: Railroads connect all of Florida's major cities, and tourism grows.

1959: Many Cubans start migrating to Florida.

1969: *Apollo 11* takes off from Cape Canaveral and lands the first man on the moon.

1971: Walt Disney World opens.

1992: Hurricane Andrew hits South Florida hard.

2011: The space shuttle *Atlantis* lifts off from Cape Canaveral in its final launch.

Activities

1. **LOCATE** the states that border Florida on the map on pages 2 and 3. Then **SAY** each state's name out loud.

2. **DESIGN** a small poster about fun things to see and do in Florida. Include words and pictures in your poster.

3. **SHARE** two facts you learned about Florida with a family member or friend.

4. **PRETEND** you are a contestant on a TV game show. The host is going to ask you five questions about Florida. If you answer correctly, you will win the game.

   a. **WHO** came from Spain and explored Florida?

   b. **WHAT** fruit does Florida grow more of than any other state?

   c. From **WHERE** did the first spaceship to land on the moon take off?

   d. **WHEN** did Walt Disney World open?

5. **UNJUMBLE** these words that have something to do with Florida. Write your answers on a separate sheet of paper.

   a. **NOGRAE** (HINT: fruit)

   b. **OPDHNIL** (HINT: An animal)

   c. **HLLES** (HINT: Something found on the beach)

   d. **IPATSRE** (HINT: They traveled by sea long ago)

   e. **PWAMS** (HINT: Alligators sometimes live there)

Glossary

airboat: a small, open boat that can travel at high speed in shallow water and swamps. (p. 4)

Ais: Native American people who once lived along the east coast of Florida. (p. 22)

Calusa: Native American people who once lived along the southwest coast of Florida. (p. 22)

coexist: live near each other peacefully. (p. 7)

egret: a large white bird with a long neck and long bill. (p. 6)

Everglades: Florida's largest wetlands; located in southern Florida. (p. 4)

Florida Keys: a chain of islands south of Florida. (p. 28)

Fountain of Youth: a mythical water spring—people believed that a drink of water from the spring would make an old person young. (p. 21)

hurricane: a powerful storm with heavy rains and winds of more than 74 miles per hour. (p. 24)

manatee: a large, slow-moving water animal that has a flipper shaped like a paddle. (p. 8)

mythical: not real, imaginary. (p. 21)

Osceola: a great leader of the Seminole people. (p. 23)

peninsula: a body of land that is surrounded on three sides by water. (p. 3)

scuba dive: to swim underwater while wearing special equipment to help you breathe compressed air from a tank on your back. (p. 28)

Seminole: a large group of Native American people who live in Florida now and are descendants of Creek people who moved to Florida in the 1700s. (p. 23)

snorkel: to swim underwater with a tube in your mouth that helps you breathe air above the water. (p. 28)

sponge: a sea animal that has a soft skeleton with many small holes that absorb water—the soft skeleton of a sponge may be used for cleaning. (p. 17)

spring: a place where underground water flows out of the ground. (p. 27)

swamp: a soft, wet area of land. (p. 4)

Tequesta: Native American people who once lived on the southeast coast of Florida. (p. 22)

Tocobaga: Native American people who once lived on the west coast of Florida. (p. 22)

tornado: a strong, whirling wind that forms a cone shape and twists in the air. (p. 25)

Answers to activities on page 34:

1) Georgia and Alabama; 2) posters will vary; 3) answers will vary; 4a) Juan Ponce de León; 4b) oranges; 4c) John F. Kennedy Space Center at Cape Canaveral; 4d) 1971; 5a) orange; 5b) dolphin; 5c) shell; 5d) pirates; 5e) swamp